a FARMYARD HEROES story

C.I. QUEST

written by Tanya Saunders

with illustrations by Faith Broomfield-Payne

The woof-woof dog and the moo-moo cow
are watching the farmer fix his plough.

"Hello, Farmer!" they call, "How are you?"
The dog barks "Woof!"
and the cow goes "Mooooooo!"

But they think the farmer has not heard,
for he does not say a single word.

In a louder, clearer voice they go,
"Hey there, Farmer!
Hello! .... Hellooooo!"

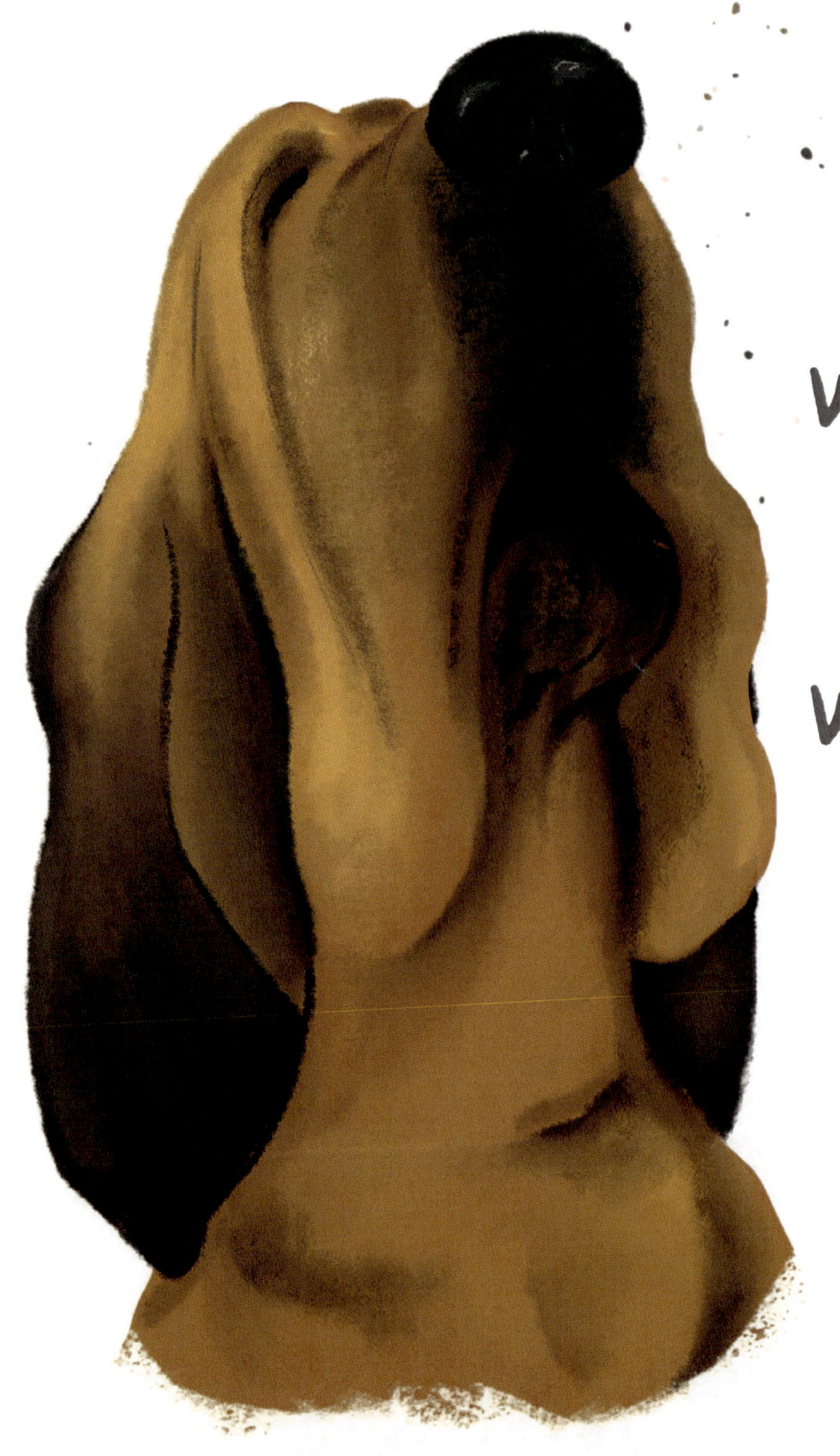

WOOF!
WOOF!
WOOF!

But still the farmer does not reply.

The dog muses, "Hmmm... I wonder why?
Maybe we should try to catch his eye."

"Or maybe the farmer cannot hear.
Are we too far away? Let's go near."

The woof-woof dog and the moo-moo cow
approach the farmer fixing his plough.

The dog barks, "Woof! Woof! Woof! Bow-wow-wow!"
"Mooooo!" says the cow, "Can you hear us now?"
But he does not move nor turn around.
He's not reacting to any sound!
"I wonder whether, by any chance,
he has lost his cochlear implants?"

"Oh no! You're right!" cries the moo-moo cow,
"I do understand the problem now...
Poor farmer! Oh dear, oh dear, oh dear!
Poor farmer! No wonder he cannot hear!"

"Both his cochlear implants are gone!"

"Has he forgotten to put them on?"

"Look at the sweat on the farmer's brow –
he's working so hard to fix his plough...
He hasn't even realised yet,
but soon he'll notice
and start to fret."

"We can't let him lose
his magic ears!

Quick! Quick! Quick!
We'll need some volunteers
before his 'ears' come to any harm!

Let's ask the animals on the farm
to join the search... to help us find them,
to look both in front and behind them...

high

and low,

up,

down,

and all around...

here, there... in the trees and on the ground!"

"No! No!" The moo-moo cow shakes her head.
"First, check the drying-box by his bed."

"I'll help you look," says the baa-baa sheep.
"Me too," says her lamb, "Bleat bleat! Bleat bleat!"

Together they spend the next few hours looking through all the grass and flowers.

BLEAT! BLEAT! BLEAT!

The handsome horse whinnies, "Neigh, neigh, neigh!
I can help! I'll look through all the hay."

NEIGH
NEIGH
NEIGH

He searches every single bale
(he even checks his water pail).

"Pfff! Pfff! Pfff!" he snorts, "It's just not fair;
I cannot find those 'ears' anywhere!"

The oink-oink pig huffs, snuffles and snorts.
"I've checked and checked my sty," she reports,
"I've searched all over, both front and rear –
the cochlear implants are not here."

COCK-A-DOODLE-DOO

They search and they search but still no luck.
"I give up," says the hen with a cluck.

"We're worried," chirp the chicks, "Cheep, cheep, cheep!"

Not so the cat, who's still fast asleep.

Zzzzzzzzzzzzz

One bold chick pokes the cat with a stick.
"Cat, please wake up, quick, quick, quick!"

Grumpily, the cat opens her eyes.
"Chicks who wake me are brave...
but not wise!"

Flap, flap, flap goes the chick as she cries,
"HELP! THE FARMER HAS LOST HIS C.I.s!"

"We're so concerned," says the sheep, "Baa! Baa! We don't know where his magic ears are!"

"Moo!" says the black and white cow, "It's true! We don't know what to do! Boo hoo hoo…"

The horse whinnies, "Neigh! Such a sad day!" and the donkey agrees, "Bray… bray… bray."

"Meeeeeeow," says the ginger cat and sighs,
"Can't you see? Have you all lost your eyes?"
She stretches, then reaches out her paw.
"Just look down!"
She points with
one sharp claw.

Everyone gasps as they see them now:
right underneath them, stuck to the plough!

The farmer's grinning from ear to ear;
"I feel much better when I can hear.
Phew! Losing my implants was no fun...
Such a relief! Clever Cat, well done!"

Everyone's smiling, even the sheep.
"Sorry, Cat, for disturbing your sleep,"
says the dog, all apologetic,
"We forgot those 'ears' are magnetic!
We should have checked everything metal:
the car, plough, tractor, fridge and kettle."

"Meow!" the farm cat smirks and replies,
"It's lucky that I've got such sharp eyes."

"It's hard to admit this," says the rat, "but three big cheers for the keen-eyed cat!"

"Hip, hip, hip! Hooray! Hooray! Hooray! The meow-meow cat has saved the day!"

Ready?

Five... four.. three... two... one... zero...

The cat is today's
FARMYARD HERO!

Let's say goodbye to all the farmyard animals:

Bye bye Dog!
WOOF WOOF WOOF

Bye bye Mouse!
SQUEAK SQUEAK SQUEAK

Bye bye Sheep!
BAA BAA BAA

Bye bye Lamb!
BLEAT BLEAT BLEAT

Bye bye Horse!
NEIGH NEIGH NEIGH

Bye bye Pig!
OINK OINK OINK

Bye bye Rooster!
COCK-A-DOODLE-DOO

Bye bye Hen!
CLUCK CLUCK CLUCK

Bye bye Chick!
CHEEP CHEEP CHEEP

Bye bye Duck!
QUACK QUACK QUACK

Bye bye Donkey!
BRAY BRAY BRAY

Bye bye Cat!
MEOW MEOW MEOW

Bye bye Rat!
GNAW GNAW GNAW

And finally, let's wave goodbye
to the farmer too:

Bye bye Farmer!

SIGN UP HERE FOR MORE BOOKS LIKE THIS →

About the Author

Tanya Saunders is Mum to twin daughters, both of whom want to be farmers (or maybe fashion designers, or vets, or teachers.) One of them wears cochlear implants – she calls them her "magic ears" because they help her to hear. (Without them, she can hear nothing at all.)
Like her daughters, Tanya loves animals. In fact, she loves them so much that it was hard for her to choose which animal to make today's farmyard hero… so she has decided to write some more Farmyard Hero stories, with a different animal saving the day each time! Watch this space…
Tanya blogs about parenting, publishing and writing at www.avidlanguage.com/hearsay-blog

About the Illustrator

the next book in the series →

As a small child you would always find **Faith Broomfield-Payne** with her nose stuck in a sketchbook or trying to create something from random items found lying around the house (a habit she hasn't really changed since then). After studying Illustration at the University of Northampton, Faith is now a professional illustrator, with a keen interest for narrative illustration. Animals are her main inspiration and she enjoys bringing out the personality of each creature she brings to life. Faith treats every piece of artwork as an experiment, never limiting herself to a certain style or concept. You can see more of her work on Instagram @faithbpillustrations

---

C.I. QUEST
Published by AVID Language Ltd., 3 Cam Drive, Ely, CB6 2WH, UK
First published in 2022

ISBN:
Paperback: 978-1-913968-17-5
Hardcover: 978-1-913968-18-2
eBook: 978-1-913968-24-3

Text © Tanya Saunders 2022
Illustrations © Faith Broomfield-Payne 2022

All rights reserved.

Also available in Spanish as "Ayudando a Bruno"
Also available in Danish as "CI Skattejagt"

Inclusive books for children with (and without) hearing loss

www.avidlanguage.com/books

Made in the USA
Middletown, DE
28 August 2024

59938448R00024

For my grandma,
who has always kept me safe
from monsters.
−F.C.

Melvina Whitmoore (More or Less a Horror Story) • Copyright © 2023 by Faith Capalia • All rights reserved • Manufactured in Italy. • No part of this book may be used or reproduced in any manner whatsoever without written permission except in the case of brief quotations embodied in critical articles and reviews • For information address HarperCollins Children's Books, a division of HarperCollins Publishers, 195 Broadway, New York, NY 10007 • www.harpercollinschildrens.com • Library of Congress Control Number: 2022943664 • ISBN 978-0-06-324782-6 • The artist used Procreate and ghostly visions to create the illustrations for this book • Typography by Caitlin E. D. Stamper • Hand lettering by Julia Christians and Faith Capalia
23 24 25 26 27 RTLO 10 9 8 7 6 5 4 3 2 1 First Edition

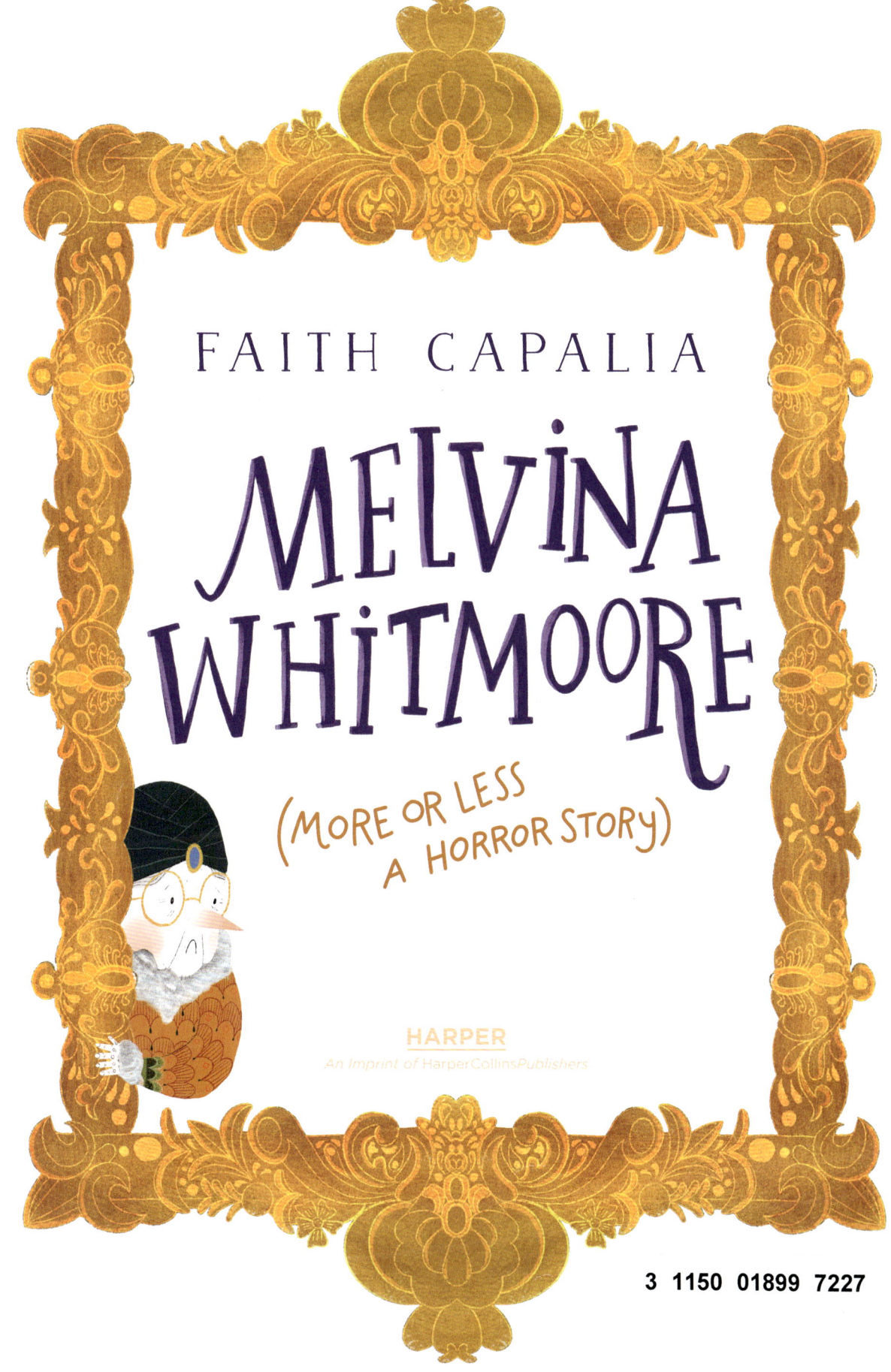

She was afraid of snails and spiders and the ticking of clocks; she was afraid of dogs and holes in the wall, of tracking mud on the carpet, and of the sound of floorboards creaking beneath her feet.

Sometimes, she was even afraid of her own **shadow**.

But when Melvina Whitmoore bought her new home on Salisbury Lane, she hoped that she had finally found somewhere safe. Nothing could ever get to her there.

As Melvina settled into her bed in her new room in her new house, she knew that she had nary a thing to fear.

Until—

Until—

The floorboards **shook** beneath her, the knob on the door began to **turn**, and the photos on the walls the walls began to **rattle**, looked like they were **alive!**

The muffled voices that bounced off the hallway walls were too loud and too many and Melvina could feel the hairs on her neck stand straight up.

Melvina tiptoed out of her bedroom and down the hallway—a massive twisting and turning place with no up and no down and where all the floorboards creaked and the walls felt alive. She climbed and crawled and eventually found herself at the end of the hallway, where she could hear shouts and hollers echoing up the looming staircase.

In her home, tracking mud across the carpet and rattling the old bones of the house were—well, Melvina didn't know quite what they were, actually. They were small and large and some had many legs and some had none and they moved in rhythm and with purpose. They seemed to be enjoying themselves!

Melvina ran as fast as she could. The creatures and critters and horrible beasts reached for her with their clawing hands and sharp talons. Melvina felt small as she scaled the looming stairs, fearful that she might slip.

Melvina dove into her bed, closed her eyes tight, and knew that here she would be safe.

However, safety is not always what we expect it to be.

"Excuse me, but we'd really like you to join your housewarming party. We didn't mean to scare you—we were just so excited to celebrate!" the skeleton rattled.

"A housewarming party?" Melvina asked.

With a delightful commotion, the monsters and beasts and ghosts and ghouls tumbled into her room, shouting and cheering.

"Of course!" said the skeleton. "This is your home, after all!"

And they were right—this was her home! Here, with her new friends and their claws and fangs and many feet, she was free to have all the fun she wanted.

Melvina had finally found somewhere safe.